CREATIVE VISUALIZATION

THE BEST VISUALIZATION TECHNIQUES AND TIPS FOR CREATIVE VISUALIZATION

ANGEL MENDEZ

CONTENTS

Introduction v
Presentation ix
Chapter 1: Creative Visualization xiii
Chapter 2: Basic Concept xvii
Chapter 3: Mild Visualization Exercises xxv
Chapter 4: Techniques for Creative Visualization xxix
Chapter 5: Taking Control xxxiii
Chapter 6: Life is a Desire xxxv
Afterword xxxvii
Conclusion xlv
Sneak Peek - Chapter 1 xlvii

©Copyright 2022 by Angel Mendez
All rights Reserved

ISBN: 978-1-63970-151-3

In no way is it legal to reproduce, duplicate, or transmit any part of this document in either electronic means or in printed format. Recording of this publication is strictly prohibited and any storage of this document is not allowed unless with written permission from the publisher. All rights are reserved.
Respective authors own all copyrights not held by the publisher.

❀ Created with Vellum

INTRODUCTION

I want to thank you and congratulate you for downloading the book *"Creative Visualization."*

This book contains proven steps and strategies on how to visualize creatively and actualize the Vision.

Visualization actuates the power of your thinking process. When you assume responsibility for your thinking process, you take responsibility for your life.

As per Emile Coue, the French psychologist, "If creative ability and willpower conflict, then perpetually it is the creative ability that wins."

It is said that words can't compare with a mental picture.
    Pictures rather than words easily influence the intuitive personality.
    The Vision or picture that we keep in our mind for a long time tends to manifest itself. Thus visualization is a speedier way for actualizing our dreams.

The entire method includes the "seeing" of your future as you need it to be. For example, if you need a new car, close your eyes and "see" yourself driving the new car.

Recall the make and model of the car, drive along known streets, "see" your companions greeting you; in short, "see" everything that will happen when you truly buy a new car.

When you visualize an idea, usually for 3-4 months, your subconscious mind will start to be sufficiently inspired to set into the opportunities or occasions to wind up in you getting your fancied car.

The Vision is appropriate for showing whatever you want, a house, another occupation, another relationship, anything.

Every one of us regularly visualizes by daydreaming. But unfortunately, the majority of us tend not to picture what we need in our life.

As we do this constantly and in continuation, for months, even for years, the desire to fulfill that need in our life gets more founded.

Rather than this, if we make Vision of success in a comparative manner, persistently (in continuation), our life will get to be prosperous with whatever we make the Vision for months or years.

Creative visualization permits us to actualize anything we dream– adoration, bliss, good relations, work satisfaction, well-being, creative imagination, inner peace, happiness, and so forth. And on and on, you can accomplish it. It's a perfect manifestation of mind over matter.

But remember, the visualization, should not be used to control or damage others.

It has been said that if this process is used to harm others, then that damage will first come to you!

Thanks again for downloading this book. I hope you enjoy it!

PRESENTATION

Creative Visualization is the art of making compelling visions and is termed as seeing with the inner consciousness.

It is a natural capability to see or sense visions in your mind - pictures of the things you covet, the life you need to lead, and the connections you desire in your life.

It is the same as wandering off in dreamland yet with a significant distinction. Wandering off in dreamland is easy and irregular, while Visualization is organized and systematic.

Some people envision in distinctive ways. Some see mental pictures as though they view a motion picture; others sense images instead of seeing them. Some sense and see the pictures at the same time.

It truly does not make a difference how you envision as long as you can actualize the vision to your intuitive personality.

Sometimes, a person may experience difficulties in envisioning. If you fall into that class, try some visualization practices or set up a Vision Board.

Creative Visualization is best utilized when you are of a positive mentality and can feel optimistic. A decent thought is to take a pleasant long hot shower, particularly around evening time, put on exceptionally relaxing music in earphones, and ponder for several minutes.

Lamentably in today's general public, it's challenging to do this at any time daily, so you can, in any event, try to meditate for five minutes the Visualization if you can't do any of other things.

After your attitude is 100% positive and relaxed, close your eyes and picture a mental film of your dream. For some individuals, it's difficult to imagine from the get-go, so use this tip.

We should say you go for a leisure time at the shoreline. Begin off with the feel, feel the warmness of the coastline and feel the light breeze coming to you continuously.

At that point, go to a hearing, hear the seagulls, the children chuckling, the individuals talking, the waves. At that point, go to seeing.

See all the individuals getting a charge out of the shoreline and see individuals tanning, swimming, snickering, making sandcastles, see the sun and the blue sky and the waves, and individuals surfing.

Now picture yourself, with all these faculties, strolling to the shoreline, taking your stuff, and doing whatever you would do at the shoreline as long as you like, albeit envisioning for short of what 5 minutes has many effects.

Creative Visualization is futile if done for 3 to 4 days in a week or something like that. Therefore, if possible, it must be carried out at any rate once a day.

While it won't harm it much if you skirt a day for a decent reason every few weeks in the vicinity, you must picture your objective daily until it happens.

You must feel like you have what you seek and envision consistently, and you must anticipate that it will happen and wait for it to happen. But, to what extent will it take?

It relies on how enormous the objective is. If you need to find out a special quill, it might just take a couple of days. If you need to get a sweetheart, it may take a week or two.

If you need to get another house or a substantial objective, it may take a couple of months. No rulebook says to what extent it will take; however, more significant goals will take longer than little ones.

CHAPTER 1: CREATIVE VISUALIZATION

Creative visualization is the technique of creating pictures in your mind and is frequently used to change toward oneself and anxiety help.

Players, famous people, and successful people from all kinds of different backgrounds have practiced creative visualization as a successful approach to enhance execution, improve aptitudes, and support trust.

As unrealistic as it may appear, creative visualization can help you overcome fears and reinforce your capacity to do anything you crave. This is because your subconscious mind accepts these dreams as genuine experiences, precisely as it would on the off chance that you were physically taking part in such a reality.

Players specifically swear by the adequacy of rationally experiencing their practices various times to upgrade their physical capabilities; however, visualization could be capable support in any try; not simply games.

Underneath, you will find out a couple of tips to help you make your visualization rehearse as compelling as could be allowed:

Make your visualizations exceptionally point by point.

Instead of just envisioning yourself in a finer circumstance than you are in now, take a stab at seeing more subtle elements of the new event you wish to experience. For instance, the sort of attire you are wearing, the size and state of your body, the other individuals around you, the points of interest of your home or profession, et cetera.

The more detail you can mix into your dreams, the more "genuine" they will appear, and the better your subconscious mind will have the capacity to accept them.

Visualize often and reliably.

Visualization is similar to any positive propensity; the benefits develop the more you do it! If you picture sporadically, your results will be similarly sporadic. Instead, set a particular time for visualization consistently, regardless of the possibility that it's just for 10 minutes.

Make it your necessity to adhere to this time except for a crisis, and you'll see it comes about significantly more rapidly.

Try to perform "small scale visualizations" a few times each day while you're going about your typical exercises. Stop for a couple of minutes, close your eyes and review a positive picture that fulfills your feel and hope about some part of your life.

Visualization help keep your center solid and minimize any pessimism you get amid the course of your ordinary schedule.

Use groups of feelings.

The emotions you experience while performing your visualization activities are more vital than the pictures you see in your brain. Case in point, in case you envision yourself as a fruitful businessman, attempt to verify you are feeling the emotions that relate to such a dream, for instance, trust, strengthening, fulfillment, and achievement!

The stronger you can make your feelings, the more compelling your visualizations will be and the more probable you will be to think and act in ways that yield them into your physical body.

CHAPTER 2: BASIC CONCEPT

Initially, visualization can influence our convictions, and convictions shape our actuality. Therefore, it is essential to have beliefs that support the objectives on which we concentrate.

Our convictions are shaped in different ways: education, family relations, media, what we read, what we watch, and our existing surroundings. When you envision you are placing yourself in the situations that you choose. Your creative visualization can influence your convictions.

For instance, say you have an open speaking occasion come up that you are anxious about, and as of now, you hold the conviction that you are a terrible speaker.

You had received that conviction in your school years when you were before the class, and you faltered while speaking—the sentence you need to change poor at open speaking. The conviction you need to impart splendid at open speaking.

With creative visualization, you can make a scene in which you are a splendid open speaker in your mind. Thus, you create a new situation that demonstrates your subconscious mind that you might be splendid at open speaking.

Rehash the visualization regularly enough, and your conviction will manifest to support what you are visioning in your mind. But our intuitive mind does not distinguish between what is occurring in our reality and what is just occurrence in our mind.

Consequently, the scene of being a splendid open speaker is exactly as true to your subconscious mind as the experience of your school time.

When the genuine day of the speech comes, you will be a splendid open speaker since your reality will reflect your convictions.

We don't require new circumstances in our lives to make new convictions as we could be responsible for what we experience in our minds.

The second reason that creative visualization might be valuable for change is that it could be a capable instrument to order the Law of Attraction.

If your vision is clear and you can see, listen, smell, taste, and touch the situation you see in your mind, you will observe that you will also candidly feel the emotions of the creative visualization.

Reality changes when we can harmonize our vibrations (feeling vitality) to the beats of what we need. The Law of Attraction lets us know that like attracts like on a vitality level.

The stronger and frequently we can feel the life we need, the sooner we will attract the desired reality. Creative visualization can place you in the passionate (vibration) state that essentially pulls in your attractions and intentions to you.

SET UP YOUR OBJECTIVE

Choose something you might want to have, progress in the direction of make or acceptance.

It could be on any level: new business or occupation, a house, a relationship, a change in yourself, improved thriving, peaceful state of mind, enhanced well-being, excellence, a better physical condition, taking care of an issue in your family or society, or whatever.

Now choose reasonably simple objectives for you to have confidence in that you feel are conceivable to acknowledge in the decently not so distant future.

That way, you won't need to manage an excessive amount of negative security in yourself, and you can augment your sentiments of accomplishment as you are learning imaginative visualization. Then, later, when you have more practice, you can assume more skilled objectives.

Make a Chosen thought or picture.

Make a vision, a mental picture, or an interest of the item or circumstance precisely as you need it. You ought to consider it in the current state as effectively existing the way you need it to be.

Envision yourself in the circumstances as you are yearning it, now. Incorporate the same number of points of interest as you can.

You may wish to make an actual physical picture of it by drawing it on the vision board. But, again, this is a nonobligatory step, not in any manner fundamental yet regularly supportive.

Concentrate on it frequently.

Bring your thought or mental picture to the mind frequently, both in calm meditative moments or in the comfortable times for the day when you happen to consider it.

It turns into a collaborative piece of your life along these lines, and it gets to be a reality for you to a greater extent.

Concentrate on it obviously, yet in a light, relaxed manner. It's critical not to feel like you are striving excessively hard for it or putting an extreme measure of vitality into it that tends to hinder instead of assistance.

Provide for its Positive Vitality

As you concentrate on your Objective, ponder it in a positive, empowering manner. Put forth tangible positive expressions to yourself: that it exists; that it has come or is currently coming to you.

See yourself accepting or attaining it. These positive articulations are termed "certifications." While you use assertions, try to incidentally suspend any questions or doubt you may have, in any event for the moment, and work on getting the inclination that what you longing for is genuine and conceivable.

Keep on living up to expectations with this method until you accomplish your Objective or no more have the longing to do so.

Keep in mind that objectives frequently change before they are accepted, which is a natural characteristic of the human process of progress and development.

So don't try to drag out it any more than you have vitality for it. If you lose interest, it may imply that now is the ideal time for another to take a gander at what you need.

If you find that an objective has changed for you, make sure to recognize that to yourself. Get clear in your mind the way that you are no more concentrating on your past Objective.

End the cycle of the old, and start the process of the new. Help you abstain from getting confounded or feeling that you've "fizzled" when you have changed.

When you accomplish an objective, please make sure to recognize intentionally to yourself that it has been finished.

Naturally, we attain things that we have been longing and picturing, and we neglect to try and recognize that we have succeeded! Therefore, to provide yourself some thankfulness and praise, and make sure to thank the Cosmos for satisfying your appeals.

Step by Step Suggestions How to Proceed?

First, determine what your aim is. It could be to change a conviction, begin loving to your beloved, become wealthy, get progress, lose weight, recuperate, to whatever you desire. Choose one and stick to it!

Consciously pick a situation that is sufficient to reflect the RESULT of your aim. Genuinely consider as this is the primary essential step. For example, if you expect to lose 30 pounds, know precisely why you need to lose the weight and how you will feel when the extra fat is gone.

Predetermine the points of interest of your situation. If it includes a festival supper, in the same way as general considerations, know which restaurant you will go to, recognize what you will wear, find the menu online and pick what you will request. Understand to the extent that you can. About your scene before you even close your eyes to envision.

If you are now toying with the conviction that your considerations make your world, you may need to peruse something propelling before starting your visualization session.

Visualization gets to be more influential if you accept that it will have any effect on your life. If you require some persuading of this conviction, take a minute to embrace it before you start.

Now you are prepared to relax! All the centered visualization starts with a brief time of relaxation. For example, you can check to count from 100 until you feel your body vanish into your surroundings, you can do dynamic muscle-relaxing beginning with your toes, and you can measure your breath.

You can feel yourself gradually sink into your cot or seat; the point is taking a couple of minutes to escape from your conscious mind so you can take advantage of your intuition.

We are significantly more open to the suggestions when rationally relaxed and calm than when our conscious innovative mind works. When you have attained this relaxed state, you will know that the incoming thoughts and feelings of your body will feel smudged. At that moment, it is strange for you!

Once you are relaxed, start observing the scene in your mind that you made prior. Go straight through from beginning to end. If you sense that you are losing center while imagining. Look, with your eyes shut, it helps to refocus yourself and keep up your state of relaxation.

Suppose you do not foreordain your situation and the more significant part of the subtle elements. In that case, it can very nearly ensure that your psyche will meander, modifying your visualization as you go, and you won't be locked in enough in the scene to interface feeling to what you are seeing.

Then the essential part of visualization, the thing that works, is to SMILE! You can't stress enough how capable grinning is to captivate your feelings in a visualization. The greater you grin, the more welled up with adoration and delight you get to be.

Permit your emotions to sparkle inside you until you have an inclination that you will power with energy.

The moment you realize that you have captivated the vitality of the Cosmos who has heard your appeal, getting your feelings included is the best way to change your convictions and change your life. The rest is simply words and pictures.

When you hit this state, you will know beyond question what it feels like to tackle your real force.

CHAPTER 3: MILD VISUALIZATION EXERCISES

Visualization exercises will help you if you are one of those unique who think that it is not easy to envision and cannot innovate creative visualization.

Creative visualization is entirely enchantment. It's simply adjusting ourselves to the laws of the Cosmos– taking the path of natural flow– and enhancing our lives with whatever we desire.

Be patient. These visualization activities will prove to be fruitful if you are customary with them.

First and foremost, choose whether you truly require these exercises. If you are a constant daydreamer, you will find visualization simple. If not, continue with these activities.

Second, you must maintain discipline. If you have concluded that you require these activities, do these activities for 2 – 3 prior weeks before plunging into creative visualization.

Find out a peaceful place where you will not be disturbed for at least 20 minutes. Bring a lemon with you. Rests or sits in a comfortable seat. Would you mind closing your eyes and calming the mind by making it of no thinking process?

To help you in this, be aware of your breathing process. Breathe in, breathe out, breathe in, and breathe out!

When the mind concentrates on breathing, it quits giving careful consideration to thoughts. And, after it's all said and done if any idea sets out to enter the mind, overlook it.

Awareness by overlooking the thinking process is powerful on account of the mind also! Therefore, managing or averting thoughts is essential as we need to save our mental energy for creative visualization.

After around two minutes of concentrating on your breathing, gradually open your eyes and observe the lemon. Note its shade, the shade of green/yellow, its shape, the surface of the skin, everything that you can note. Likewise, smell it. Let the reviving emanation of lemon fill your nostrils and get into your mind.

Now close your eyes and try to "see" the lemon. Recreate it precisely as you saw it. Color, shape, composition & smell! If you think that it difficult, open your eyes again and take another gander at the lemon. Smell it once more.

Now close your eyes and try to envision the lemon. Proceed with this activity till you can see and smell the lemon with your closed eyes.

When you are indeed fit to see and feel the lemon in your inner being, the first of your visualization activities is finished. This may take one day, two days, or more. It depends on person to person. So be that as it may be steady till you succeed.

Relax for some time! Again, close your eyes and see the car you had always wanted. It helps if you have a photograph of the vehicle and take a test ride of that car.

Keep in mind that smooth drive, the interest of the steering wheel in your grasp, the composition of the calfskin situates, the influential murmur of the motor, the sound of shutting the door, and other possibilities that you loved in the car.

Try to recollect however many things as would be prudent about the car, for example, shade, musical sound of the horn, et cetera. Then, when you open your eyes, you ought to feel as though you have driven ventures out of the car.

You can devise a lot of situations of such visualization practices yourself. Anyway, don't get excessively involved in visualization works out.

Begin imagining your goals as quickly as time permits. Careful discipline brings about promising results! The more visualization you improve, the more you get to be gaining fruitful results.

CHAPTER 4: TECHNIQUES FOR CREATIVE VISUALIZATION

Creative Visualization is an aptitude that implies that everybody can learn it and enhance it through practice. It is the capacity to envision things.

This skill includes innovativeness and creative ability.
Thus, enhancing Visualization will enhance the other two related aptitudes the more prominent the points of interest of the mental pictures you make, the more pronounced the expertise.

Creative Visualization is a unique imperative capacity that you may have to extend your mind. It is the most apparent element for fruitful self-mesmerizing.

The absence of it will not let you move towards the transform you need to do in yourself. So, as we now comprehend the power of Visualization, we should see some essential visualization works out.

In the first place, consider something you would like. Then, for this activity, pick something simple that you can undoubtedly envision achieving.

It may be a system you might want to have, an occasion you might want to have happened, a circumstance in which you would like to end up, or some condition in your life you would like to progress.

Get in a comfortable position, either sitting or resting, in a calm spot where you will not be irritated. Relax your body. Beginning from your toes and climbing to your scalp, consider relaxing each muscle in your body. Thus, it is letting every one of the strain streams out of your body.

Inhale profoundly and gradually from your gut. Number down slowly from ten to one, inclination you are getting more profoundly loose with each tally.

When you feel deeply relaxed, begin to envision what you need as you would like it. If it is an item, imagine yourself with the article, use it, appreciate it, get a charge out of it, and reveal it to companions.

If it is a circumstance or occasion, envision yourself there and everything occurrence precisely as you need it. For example, you may visualize what individuals are stating or any points of interest that make it more genuine to you.

You may take a generally brief time or very much a couple of moments to envision this, whatever feels best to you.

Mess around with it. It ought to be an altogether pleasant experience, in the same way as a tyke wandering off in fantasy land about what he needs for his birthday.

Now keeping the thought or picture still in your mind, rationally make some exceptionally positive, confirmed articulations to yourself (calmly) about it, for example,

Here I am, using a glorious weekend in the mountains. What a delightful get-away.

I cherish the perspective of my roomy, new condo.
 I'm figuring out how to love and accept myself as I am.
 These positive instances, termed as called insistences, are a vital piece of creative visualization!
 Finally, if you like, you can end your visualization with the firm articulation to yourself:
 or something better now shows in ultimately fulfilling and congruous courses.

This practice leaves space for something else and far and away superior to what you had initially imagined. It serves as an update to you that this procedure capacities for the shared benefits of all.

If questions or opposing considerations emerge, do not avoid them or attempt to counteract them, this will tend to provide for them a force they don't generally have.

Let them move through your awareness, recognize them, and return to your positive proclamations and pictures.

Do this method just if you think that it is charming and intriguing. It could be five minutes or thirty minutes. Rehash consistently or as regularly as possible.

As you see, the essential process is moderately simple. Using it truly viably, on the other hand, generally obliges some understanding and refinement.

CHAPTER 5: TAKING CONTROL

Not everybody accepts they can take complete control of their lives. Some people would say there are some hindrances in their future, and they like it that way or take after Supreme every day to provide for them heading.

Although this is likewise paramount to understand that much of who we are every day need to do with the decisions we make.

For the individual who needs to know why the way appears to go in rounds, heading to no place, there is the esteem in having the capacity to envision circumstances that have preferred conclusions over the ones they experience at this time.

With creative visualization, individuals are taught to envision themselves, their lives, their prospects. They see who they need to be, occupations, a wish to be doing, and victories on what they will delight.

These pictures could include adoring connections, professional advancements, lives with less stress, and surroundings of more prominent excellence.

Frequently the best obstructions people face are their contrary state of mind. They sense that they can't succeed, so instead of looking ahead, they take a gander at their feet.

No big surprise they tumble down. When you show a kid to walk or ride a bicycle, you likely let him know to look straight ahead: you go where you look. Find and away from the objective you have as a primary concern, and that is the place your feet will take you.

CHAPTER 6: LIFE IS A DESIRE

Creative Visualization is not a beyond any doubt fire approach to dependably win the following enormous soccer amusement, benefit, or win over the affection of your life, all by itself, as different applications are required alongside it much of the time.

Occasionally, you are not bound for the precise results you envision, yet the results may be far superior to what you expected.

Likewise, the key here is to envision, not simply picture. It would be best if you used your creative ability to fortify your dreams.

It would help if you took pictures in your brain out of trusts and dreams which have not yet worked out as expected. They must be occupied entirely with sentiments and settings. The more genuine you make them, the more achievable they will appear.

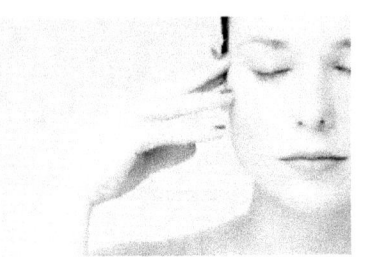

AFTERWORD

The significant benefits of Creative Visualization are that it helps you to get a more considerable amount of what you need.

When you vividly envision attaining your objectives, you enhance an entire arrangement of intuitive courses of action to help you achieve your target.

Out goes "determination" - supplanted by "smooth achievement".

Via "preparing your mind" to recognize what you need, you will unavoidably experience more "genuine" achievement - and feel more chilled about the technique, as well.

That is right, you as of now "envision" - presumably without knowing it!

You see, every & each time you stress over the future, get restless about what may happen, or persuade yourself that times are "bad."

You are envisioning just about the wrong things!

When you intentionally visualize the circumstances you WANT instead, you recover control over your experience. You will feel more positive & hopeful, as well.

Alpha waves are staggering bravo, and when your mind produces them, you experience enhanced relaxation, centering & joy, and decrease torment, stress & nervousness.

When you envision legitimately, your mind produces Alpha Waves - purpose, aside from helping shape your dream life, you get to be healthier at the same time!

"Your intuitive can't differentiate between a true memory and a vividly envisioned visualization."

All things considered, when you envision you viably "embed" new memories into your mental self-view, implying that your subconscious mind "thinks you are the achievement you long for being

arranges for subconscious assets to help you achieve your objectives, and it likewise expands certainty, here and there significantly, pretty much the best "deceive" you can ever play on yourself!

One of the benefits of visualization is that it's amusing to envision yourself - in incredible subtle element - performing taking care of Your goal!

Visualization is helpful for anybody's conscience!

When it's all said and done, who wouldn't have any desire to envision carrying on with their fantasy life - in rich, vivid, subtle elements?

After a couple of days of Creative Visualization, you will begin to feel confident (basically since you've polished achievement in your mind for a long time).

The more specific you are, the more open doors you see and the more achievement you will experience, which is a definitive ethical ring!

That is why Olympic competitors, film stars, golfers, ballplayers, top deals superstars & tip-top agents use Creative Visualization to enhance the results.

When you imagine, you make new neural pathways in your mind. Then, when you repeatedly do this, your mind "recalls" the practical activity and making it much simpler for you to experience accomplishment seriously.

Mental practice sets you up for the "genuine article" - and the more vivid and "life-like" your visualizations, the progressively you will find that your intuitive personality assumes control when you have to do your thing!

Look around you. All that you see began life as an IDEA in somebody's mind.

The physical structure ALWAYS takes after a thought.

So why not go straight to the workshop which creates EVERYTHING - the mind and begin making a few manifestations of your own?

Moreover, unless you envision something inside your brain in VIVID, a subtle element, you will not see it "out there" in this world.

So that is the reason you got to "Think rich" before you might BE rich.

When you vividly envision carrying on with your fantasy life, you do yourself extraordinary support:

You supplant alarm & conventionalism with probability & want.

You get a sight of yourself performing, getting it done, accomplishing your maximum capacity.

In short, this is ESPECIALLY useful for the soul.

You will feel recharged, with expanded vitality and a feeling of reason.

Another benefit of creative visualization is that each one time you Visualize, you will develop highly serene and profoundly relaxed.

Might you be able to do with some more "Zen" in your life?

In time, you'll anticipate your Visualizations to the extent that the profound peace you accomplish for the delight of making what you need in life!

In today's manic world, this will genuinely chill you out.

The more you picture, the more centered you'll be, and the more yearning you'll create for making your objectives happen as the more you picture, the more centered you'll be, and the more yearning you'll create for making your objectives happen as expected.

Visualization will help you to be as centered as you have ever been.

Furthermore, as Napoleon Hill notes in Think & Grow Rich,

a "definiteness of reason" coupled with yearning makes wealth (of any sort!)

Try to visualize for a couple of weeks. At that point, recognize the amount more determined - and beneficial - you are.

When you visualize, you will get thoughts & hunches to help you defeat your difficulties.

By vividly envisioning what to do, you will experience bits of knowledge that help to get you once more on track when you experience barricades on the way to achievement.

All from the solace of your room!

Your subconscious mind is overwhelmed with directions to take after - so it truly gets to work! You will be astounded at how "innovative" you are.

With proceeded of practice, plans begin flying into your brain at an alarming rate!

You will realize what to do and how to do it.

Also, for the times when you inevitably "destroy," you will get thoughts to get you again on track expected.

Visualization will help you to be as centered as you have ever been.

Furthermore, as Napoleon Hill notes in Think & Grow Rich, a "definiteness of reason" coupled with yearning makes wealth (of any sort!)

Try to visualize for a couple of weeks. At that point, recognize the amount more determined - and beneficial - you are.

When you visualize, you will get thoughts & hunches to help you defeat your difficulties.

By vividly envisioning what to do, you will cxperience bits of knowlcdge that help to get you once more on track when you experience barricades on the way to achievement.

All from the solace of your room!

Your subconscious mind is overwhelmed with directions to take after - so it truly gets to work! You will be astounded at how "innovative" you are.

With proceeded of practice, plans begin flying into your brain at an alarming rate!

Finally, you will realize what to do and how to do it.

Also, for the times when you inevitably "destroy," you will get thoughts to get you again on track.

It would be best if you put the plans into practice.

When you are in Alpha, you get to a higher nature of thought, far from the regularly befuddled pushing of Beta.

After a couple of days of deliberately getting to Alpha, you will recognize a "flying creature's eye perspective" of all your issues, objectives & plans. You will be in a significantly improved educated position to make a move on them, as well.

You will feel more "in order" with what to do.

Furthermore, less fretted over "what could happen"!

It feels VERY decent to envision - in vivid point of interest - being rich and super-fruitful.

In addition, as specified over, your subliminal begins to "accept" that you genuinely are rich as of now!

This creates a "flourishing cognizance," which all the Wealth Gurus and is fundamental to making accomplishments of any sort.

Provide for it a go. It sounds insane. However, I think it works. The "richer" I feel, the more cash I gain.

The last of the benefits of visualization is maybe the most essential.

Inspiring, effective pictures on your intuitive DOES enhance your mental self-view, which brings about feeling more satisfied, more skilled, and surer.

Try visualization for a couple of days to see what happens.

You will, likely, begin to feel as sure & confident as you have been a significant part of your life. Furthermore, the profits of visualization show signs of improvement with time.

You will feel like you at best, however, more regularly.

Most likely a considerable measure more!

CONCLUSION

I hope this book was able to help you to imagine yourself showing signs of improvement. You can envision your body modifying itself, and as such, your body will start to react.

The other benefit is that the demonstration of picturing, regardless of your imagining, diminishes stress, unwinds the brain, and expands our general inclination, thus bringing down our circulatory strain and permitting our body to capacity at the total limit.

Imagine something that you need to have or need to experience to bring extraordinary euphoria into your life.

We may not be in the position to do or have what we need. However, we can imagine it, and it is the following best thing to having it or doing it.

Our brains do not have the most straightforward idea about the distinction between visualization and having or doing something. So, it will react in the same way it would if you were experiencing that which you are imagining.
The End.

Did you like this book? Then you'll LOVE Lucid Dreaming

Master The Best Techniques for Lucid Dreaming, OBE, and Astral Projection

You're about to discover a proven strategy on how to use the best techniques for lucid dreaming and OBE so that you can experience and create an extraordinary dream life

In this book, you will learn how to master the art of lucid dreaming with the best techniques I have learned

This incredible book will teach you how to use lucid dreams to create your ideal world, overcome fears, improve creativity, meet anybody you want, create imaginary characters to help you solve any problem, naturally heal yourself, be able to fly, travel through time and much more.

With Lucid Dreaming our dream world is a world of infinite possibilities.

People spend more than half their life sleeping and by effectively Lucid Dreaming and OBE as taught in this book

we can take advantage of all this time and get the right insights, boost our creativity, heal ourselves emotionally, mentally, spiritually, and whatever way you can think of.

Just imagine, no limits. And as a result, to use the special Lucid Dreaming techniques in this book you will live a more fulfilling life in both your dream world and your conscious life.

Lucid Dreaming: The Best Lucid Dreaming Techniques and Tips for OBE and Lucid Dreaming

https://books2read.com/u/b5XJzl

SNEAK PEEK - CHAPTER 1

Lucid Dreaming: The Best Lucid Dreaming Techniques and Tips for OBE and Lucid Dreaming

https://books2read.com/u/b5XJzl

———

Lucid dreaming is mindfulness that you are imagining. This mindfulness can go from an extremely swoon distinction of reality to something as manifestation as the growth of awareness past what has ever been accomplished, even in waking life.

Lucid dreams naturally happen while an individual is amidst a consistent dream and suddenly aware that they are dreaming. When you understand this, you will control your dreams, which is essentially the most basic part of lucid dreaming.

CHAPTER 1

What does "LUCID DREAM" mean?

Despite the fact that the expression "lucid" means clear, lucid dreaming is more than simply having a normal dream. To have a lucid dream, you must realize that it's a fantasy while you're dreaming. That is it.

It doesn't oblige that you can control anything in your dream, however, control is the thing that starting lucid visionaries frequently go for. Individuals get pulled into lucid dreaming on the grounds that they need to have the capacity to do things they could never do in waking reality, for instance, fly to the sky.

More accomplished lucid visionaries understand the benefits of clear imagining. You can utilize it to investigate the limits of your mind and the unlimited parts of the universe.

What's the best process for getting to be lucid in dreams?

The best process for getting to be LUCD is to be more aware and look and listen and give careful consideration to points of interest, as when you see things that don't fit, that is an intimation that you're imagining.

To encourage the process, you can structure the propensity of analyzing nature's domain or your state of awareness amid the day. For example, mental propensities you work on amid the day have a tendency to proceed in dreams.

So you analyze your surroundings amid the day, you look at your mindfulness, and afterward, you may perceive that something is diverse once you begin imagining. Somebody who has gotten to be clear has much larger amounts of mindfulness, and clearly, Ii is found that is one of the greatest benefits of lucid dreaming.

A Dream isn't clear unless you control it!

There is some disarray about the distinction in the middle of clarity and dream control. The two are connected; however, one can happen without the other. Still, some of the lucid dreams experience almost no control in a few instances. Then again, it is conceivable to practice some fantasy control without being mindful that it is a fantasy. Normally the fantasy plot will clarify this by making the visionary accept divine control over everything. Dream control, by our definition, could be either conscious or oblivious.

Lucid dreaming is New Age

Since we all have clear dreams commonly now and then, we realize that any one perspective does not constrain clear envisioning.

There are verifiable records which discuss clear imagining doing a reversal a large number of years- -so it is scarcely another sensation. There is no compelling reason to have any profound convictions to revel in clear dreams.

Clear imagining Supporters' Idealism

Lucid dreaming happens while you are sleeping; it is not implied at all to infringe upon your inclusion in this present reality. While numerous clear visionaries appreciate recording their fantasies, discussing their fantasies, and arranging fun clear dreams, this is, for the most part, the same as another distraction.

Truth be told, playing a feature amusement or viewing a motion picture will take you out of "this present reality" more than clear envisioning will.

Clear imagining is unique & includes Mysterious

Numerous religious or spiritual groups' are protuberance of clear imagining in with mysterious practices and exercises. On the other hand, transparent dreams regularly happen commonly, and there is nothing mysterious about them.

Numerous extraordinary religious epiphanies and messages came as dreams; in some cases, clear dreams. Our dreams are what we make them; whether we wish to provide for them profound centrality or not is dependent upon us.

Dreams contain messages that are lost with Lucid Dreaming

As of this composition, there are numerous speculations concerning why dreams exist and what reason they serve, but none of these hypotheses have been demonstrated so far.

One hypothesis is that our fantasies contain important or helpful messages about our lives. Considering that numerous individuals don't significantly recall their fantasies without considering changing the fantasy plot in a small amount's one had always wanted is in examination not almost as risky for any message-sending done through dreams.

Lucid dreaming requires great dream review regardless of the possibility that a small amount of these messages are lost in clear dreams.

You are likely recollecting a lot of more normal dreams than you ever did some time recently, and on top of that, providing for them more consideration than at any other time.

Levels of Lucidity & Dream Control

Clear imagining was characterized as getting to be mindful.

The genuine level of mindfulness shifts, on the other hand. When clarity is high, you are well mindful that nothing you encounter is true, and you understand that you don't have anything to fear. You can't be hurt by any circumstances that may appear unstable.

With low-level clarity, even though somewhat mindful you are imagining, you are not mindful enough to have an incredible effect on your dream. You may accept a few parts of your dreams that you would not naturally accept in the routine.

With low-level clarity, your acknowledgment might additionally rapidly blur, and you may acknowledge the entire dream as reality.

A lucid dream is a regular and sound experience. It is much like another dream aside from the little distinction of your information that it is a fantasy. It has nothing to do with the new age, the mysterious, or idealism, nor would it be able to damage you any more than a consistent dream could.

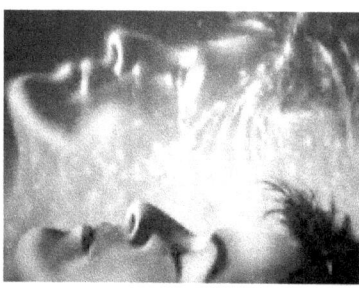

Keep a dream journal close by your cot during the evening, and compose in it quickly in the wake of waking. On the other hand, you can keep a recording gadget off chance that you think it is simpler to rehash your fantasy so everyone can hear.

This helps you perceive your regular dream components (individuals from your past, particular spots, and so on.), furthermore tells your mind that you are not kidding about recalling your fantasies!

It will additionally help you to perceive things that are one of a kind to your fantasies. You will have the capacity to perceive your own "fantasy signs." These will be repeating things or occasions that you may recognize in your fantasies.

By being mindful of your slumber plan, you can organize your example to help actuate clear dreams.

Concentrates on determinedly recommend that a snooze a couple of hours in the morning wake is the most widely recognized time to have a clear dream.

Lucid dreams are unequivocally connected with REM rest. REM sleep is condensed just before the last wakening. This implies they most usually happen just before waking up.

CHAPTER 2

Astral Projection

Astral projection helps a state of profound relaxation, so it ought to be performed in a place of your home where you're comfortable. Lie on your couch and relax your mind and body.

It's simpler to perform astral projection alone than it is with another person in the room. So if you comfortably rest with an accomplice, pick a room other than the room to practice astral projection.

Draw the shades or draperies and free the room of hindering commotions. Any kind of interference could upset the state of relaxation you have to attain.

Position yourself on your back in your picked room. Shut your eyes and try to clear your mind of diverting thinking processes. Focus on your body and how it feels. The objective is to accomplish a state of complete mind and body relaxation.

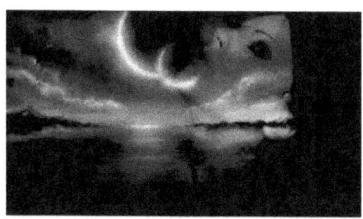

Flex your muscles and then slacken them. Begin with your toes and work your path up to your body, step by step going to your head. Be sure that each muscle is loose when you are through.

Inhale profoundly and breathe out totally. Don't hold pressure in your chest and shoulders. Simply relax.

Center your mind on your relaxing. Don't escape with thoughts of outside stresses, and don't get distracted with the thought of your soul anticipating from your body. Instead, simply let yourself sink into relaxation.

This entrancing state is typically known as the hypnogogic state. Let your body and mind method rest, yet don't lose consciousness. Being at the edge of awareness and sleep, a mesmerizing state is essential for astral projection to happen

Achieve this state using the below-mentioned technique:

Keeping your eyes closed, let your mind meander to a part of your body, for instance, your hand, foot, or a solitary toe.

Concentrate on the body part until you can envision it impeccably, even with your eyes closed. Then, keep concentrating until all different thoughts fall away.

Use your brain to flex your body part. However, don't physically move it. For example, envision your toes twisting and uncurling or your fingers holding and unclenching until it appears to be as if they are physically moving.

Grow your awareness to other parts of your body. Move your legs, your arms, and your head using just your mind. Keep your center relentless until you're ready to move your entire body in your mind alone.

Some people report feeling vibrations, which come in waves at various frequencies, as the soul gets ready to leave the body. Don't be perplexed about the vibrations since the vicinity of alarm may make you leave your meditative state; rather, succumb to the vibrations as your soul gets ready to leave your body.

Envision in your mind the room in which you are lying. Move your body in your brain to remain up. Look around yourself. Get up off the informal lodging over the room, then turn around and take a gander at your body on the couch.

Your awareness is effective if you feel as if you are looking upon your body from over the room and that your conscious self is now separate from your body.

It takes a considerable time of practice to get to this point. If you experience difficulty-totally lifting your soul from your body, take a stab at lifting simply a hand or a leg right away. Then, continue rehearsing until you're equipped to move over the room.

Your soul dependably stays united with your body with undetectable energy once in a while, alluded to as a Silver Rope. Let the power manage your soul again to your body. Reemerge your body. Move your fingers and toes physically, not just in your mind, and let yourself recapture full awareness.

When you have aced the demonstration of anticipating your soul from your body in the same room, you will need to affirm that you were indeed in two different planes.

Next time you practice astral projection, don't turn around to take a gander at your body. Instead, leave the room and stroll into another room of your home.

Look at an item in the other room, something that you had never recognized previously in the physical sense. Make a mental note of its shade, shape, and size, carefully considering whatever a number of subtle elements could be allowed.

Come back to your body. Physically go into the room you beforehand anticipated yourself into. Stroll to the article you analyzed during the astral travel.

Will you affirm the points of interest you noted when you investigated the item with your mind?

During consequent astral projection sessions, go to areas that are unique to you. Each one time, note subtle elements that you had never perceived previously. After every session, physically confirm the points of interest.

After a couple of outings, you will be accomplished enough to go to areas that are new to the trust that you have really performed astral projection.

Some say that astral projection is unsafe, particularly when one gets enough practice to investigate new places. However, it is pleasant to envision yourself showered in a shining- Silver White Light before your astral undertaking.

Envision it as a sky around you; this will secure you from other thinking processes. However, there is such a great amount to get into. Realize that no damage will come to you unless you think it will. The rush of having an awareness keeps some individuals out of their bodies for long times of time, which is said to debilitate the silver line.

End of Sneak Peek

Lucid Dreaming: The Best Lucid Dreaming Techniques and Tips for OBE and Lucid Dreaming

https://books2read.com/u/b5XJzl

©Copyright 2022 by Angel Mendez
All rights Reserved
In no way is it legal to reproduce, duplicate, or transmit any part of this document in either electronic means or in printed format. Recording of this publication is strictly prohibited and any storage of this document is not allowed unless with written permission from the publisher. All rights are reserved. Respective authors own all copyrights not held by the publisher.

Created with Vellum

www.ingramcontent.com/pod-product-compliance
Lightning Source LLC
LaVergne TN
LVHW021738060526
838200LV00052B/3337